Microsoft SharePoint Interview Questions, Answers and Explanations

by Terry Sanchez-Clark

ITCOOKBOOK

Microsoft SharePoint Questions, Answers and
Explanations: Microsoft SharePoint Interview Questions
1-933804-66-1

by Terry Sanchez-Clark
Edited by Emilee Newman Bowles

Printed in the United States of America

TABLE OF CONTENTS

Introduction

If you are a subscriber to the theory that *The World is Flat* then the genesis of this book should not come as a surprise to you. This book was born because there is an increasing number of people collaborating across international boundaries, and hence and increased demand for Microsoft SharePoint professionals worldwide. And also because we think that Sharepoint is an important piece of software. True, it is simple, but it can capture a very important work function and we believe it is a great tool for businesses. Sharepoint enables what I consider to be a very elegant and simple workflow system. In fact, at Equity Press we use Sharepoint for our publishing operation to gather, track, and collaborate on all of the various aspects of our book publishing business.

If you are a newcomer to the world of SharePoint – welcome. If you are an experienced user, we hope that this book serves as a handy guide, a quick reference, a cookbook that you can refer to from time to time to help you out on the job.

What is SharePoint?

SharePoint allows you to create custom views of the content management web site. This customization can be very simple or very complex, depending on the type and version of the product that is installed. In addition, Share Point has a powerful collaboration model that is tightly integrated with the Office 2003 suite.

The current version of Share Point is its seventh. Like most Microsoft software, version 3 was the version to gain rapid adoption. A recent article in the register indicated that

Share Point Portal Server is Microsoft's fastest growing product, with 30 million licenses.

History of SharePoint

Microsoft's first portal application was called Digital Dashboard. This product introduced the concept of web parts; boxes of information on a page that represented a summary or overview of information. By assembling multiple parts on a page, each user could customize his view of the portal to contain the information that pertained to him. In theory, every visitor of the site could have different content at the same URL. However, the technology behind the Digital Dashboard was not up to the task, and it never made it out of the beta stage.

At the same time, Microsoft's Office group was working toward a collaboration solution. The need for many people to contribute to a single document or worksheet was growing. And these people were not necessarily working at the same location. The result was Share Point Team Services (STS), a web-based solution that allowed shared access to information and documents. STS also allowed end-users to make changes to the site via a web browser instead of requiring a development-oriented application.

The merging of the collaboration and aggregation functions lead to Share Point Portal Server 2001. Portal Server has been upgraded to run on the .Net framework and is now referred to as Share Point Products and Technologies. The "Product" is Share Point Portal Server 2003 (SPS) and the "Technologies" are Windows Share Point Services (WSS). A significant point about these two is that WSS is included with the Windows Server 2003 license. Any organization that is licensed for Windows Server 2003 can also host websites that are based on WSS.

Features of Share Point

In general, Share Point contains all of the features you would expect from a portal or collaboration tool:

- Browser-based customization of pages.
- Browser-based content administration.
- Aggregation capabilities.
- Document repository.
- Message board.
- Ad-hoc data storage.
- E-mail notifications.
- Announcements, event calendar and contact list.

A complete feature matrix that also indicates whether the feature is part of WSS or SPS can be found in the whitepaper Implementing Rich Collaboration Infrastructure using Windows Share Point Services and Share Point Portal Server 2003 on Microsoft's web site. (http://www.microsoft.com/sharepoint/evaluationovervie w.asp).

Uses for Share Point

In addition to being the default intranet portal, there are many additional uses for Share Point. Microsoft has included pre-defined templates for Web sites to facilitate meetings, manage projects and create documents combined with the "self-service" site creating feature, teams can create and use a web site with minimal assistance from the Information Technology Department.

The Document Workspace template will allow a group to work on a document. The template combines a document repository with a task list and a links list. While using Word 2003, a user can have the document open and at the same time view the task or links list. Changes made to the task list are immediately visible to site visitors. And the document library allows versioning, so edits are not lost.

The Meeting Workspace template combines the agenda, attendee list and Outlook's calendar function. When sending a meeting request in Outlook 2003, a user can create a workspace on the server. The URL of the workspace is automatically included in the message and the attendees are added to the site. The materials required for the meeting can be centrally located, which is preferable for attendees who travel frequently.

The browser-based customization feature, combined with the ability to create ad-hoc lists, allows an advanced user to create a site for almost any purpose.
A user group could host its meeting schedule, complete with handouts. A youth sport organization can post its schedule and roster. An individual can host a blog.

Question 1: Share Point Installation

We are having a problem with the installation of Share Point.

We have IIS set to Digest Authentication and the web configuration file has impersonate set to true and the authentication mode set to Windows.

Every time a user goes to the site, they are prompted for their window's login details. They enter their network username and password and that gets them access to the site.

The user is already logged onto the network with those credentials though, so why do they have to type them in again? Is there something I am missing?

A: Share Point added their sites to the Local or Trusted Zone in Internet Explorer to get around the user credential prompt, but we are running NTLM as an authentication method. You could put it in Intranet Zone if you also checked the radio button to use the current username and password.

Question 2: Renaming a Domain

I am planning to rename our domain and we are using the Share Point Portal Server.

Does anyone know if this will have any effect on Share Point?

A: I think you will run into problems. I did some testing a while back both with domain name change and port number change in Share Point. I was able to run Share Point but there were also things that did not work like indexing. It also stopped working when installing web parts.

It is possible to change, but it might require a lot of work. I did change port numbers on the website in IIS and that also made Share Point behave strangely. I am not sure that the Share Point configuration database is updated when making a name or port change.

So I would try and test it in a demo environment before trying with a production environment.

Before you physically change the domain name or port number for Share Point Server, you need to do the backup and restore the method. This is due to the configuration database having links to the server hard coded resulting in broken functionalities in at least the search tool.

Question 3: Restoring Databases

I have backup of both the configuration and contents database. I want to restore them to a new server running Share Point and recover the original Share Point site.

How can I do this?

A: Do the following steps:

1. Take the SQL ba ckup file that creating the live content database and moved it onto the new DR server.

2. Then setup the Share Point site again on the new server.

3. Restore the backup database over the new content database on the DR server, then detach it and re-attach it from Share Point. This will re-create the site.

4. Finally, re-apply indexing to re-create the search index.

Question 4: WSS Over SSL

I want to host a WSS site over SSL. My ISP will only enable port 443 on the firewall.

Will external clients be able to view the site with that alone? Or do I also need a TCP port opened?

A: It should be enough. SSL runs on TCP port 443 (by default) so that should work. You also need to install a certificate on your web server.

Question 5: "Fill Out This Form" Button

I am receiving a dialog box stating that "This feature requires Microsoft Internet Explorer 5.0 or later and a Windows Share Point Services-compatible XML editor such as Microsoft Office InfoPath."

It works when I run it in Internet Explorer, but the company prefers Firefox. And using InfoPath is required by management.

Is there a way to get the "fill out this form" button in Share Point Form libraries to work using Firefox?

A: Share Point was designed to run on MS Office stack. This means that it works best if you have Office 2003, InfoPath 2003, FrontPage 2003, IE6, Active Directory, Exchange Server, and BizTalk.

And Firefox is not yet a supported browser to use with Share Point. There are a couple of things that do not work at all with FireFox and Share Point. Windows Share Point Services is compatible with an XML editor such as Microsoft Office InfoPath.

Question 6: Removing Edit in Microsoft Office Word

I want to remove the Edit in Microsoft Office Word feature from the drop down list in the document library. I would rather have individuals check out and check in documents.

How can I accomplish this?

A: The place in the file system of the front end web server where WSS keeps all its feature files is:

C:\program files\common files\Microsoft shared\web server extensions\12\template\features

I know that you can add things to menus there. Try and modify these files to remove them.

Question 7: Moving To a New Database Server

Does anyone know the proper procedure for moving from one database server to another?

Here's an example:

Share Point was installed using MSDE. Usage has increased and now we need to migrate to a dedicated SQL Server machine.

I have done some digging but the instructions I have found stated that you need to disconnect from the content database and configuration database and re-connect to the new server after restoring the backup. Is this true?

A: Partly yes and no. Even though you have disconnected the content and configuration databases, removing, and re-installing the Share Point Services onto the virtual server, you should still re-initialize the database connections.

This does not mean you "Add/Remove Programs" Share Point Services. You only remove the virtual Share Point "site" from the IIS virtual server and then set it up again pointing to the new locations.

Note: Disconnecting the databases can't do it. You probably need to remove the virtual server first.

Question 8: Web Services in MOSS 2007

Where can I find all the web services available in MOSS 2007? I have the list for Share Point Service 2003. I would like to know whether it is still the same with any new services being added.

A: The Share Point web services can still be found in the _vti_bin folder.

```
(c:\Program Files\Common Files\Microsoft Shared\web server
extensions\12\ISAPI).
```

Just have a look.

There are extra Web Services, like for workflow, the business data catalog, etc.

You can find some basic information in the SDK's:

- WSS 3.0 SDK: Introduction to the Windows Share Point Services Web Service.

- MOSS SDK: Web Services Overview.

Question 9: Impersonation Problem in Share Point

We are trying to grant temporary rights to the connected user in order to use a Share Point method that demands administrator privileges, such as creating Share Point Webs, Share Point Lists, and Share Point List Items or to retrieve the Welcome Page of a Share Point Web.

It did not work in classical impersonate method used in Share Point Service 2003. We thought that it was the problem of the "Roles retrieval" in Share Point Service 2003, which forces the use of AppDomains. But this solution is not suitable because everything we try causes an Access Denied Exception.

When we impersonate, the Windows Identity associated to the context correctly becomes the AppPool Identity (checked with Debug). But it seems that the security context, on which MOSS is based, is still the users' one checked by using its API: for example, SPContext.Current.Web.CurrentUser is a SPUser corresponding to the one it is connected to. This seems to have the consequence that even in an impersonated block, if we create a new list, the creator of the list is the logon user, not the current user.

How do I make this work? Am I forgetting something?

A: You can try the following:

```
SPSite site = new SPSite(url);

SPWeb web = site.OpenWeb();

web.RootFolder.WelcomePage, etc.
```

Also make sure you run the code with elevated privileges.

Question 10: Creating a Web Part

I want to create a web part with content scrolling on it just like news scrolling on the panel from bottom to up.

How can I do this?

A: The easy way is to insert a stroller is by using the <marquee> html element:

```
<marquee width="50 %">

Lorem ipsum dolor sit amet, consectetuer adipiscing elit.

</marquee>
```

Alternatively, you can use JavaScript:
http://www.widomaker.com/~reboughner/W3C/scrollban ner/scroll.html

```
.NET & Share point developer
www.peoplenet.dk
```

Note that the marquee tag is only supported by the most recent versions of browsers. It is a fairly new tag, not part of HTLM 3.2 and older. So if you use it, check how it performs in different browsers.

Question 11: Binding Share Point to ASP.NET

How can I bind a Share Point list to an ASP.NET view control like Data Grid, Details View, and Data List?

I have created an ASPX page with a Details View ASP.NET control and all my code is written in-line between script blocks on the same ASPX page (HTML View). After I saved the file, I uploaded the ASPX page to one of the Document Libraries I have on my Share Point Site.

I can build the list object through code but I can't seem to display the custom columns or properties. All I can display is the stock properties/columns that come with any list: ID, Display Name, and Title, etc. But if I added a new column to that list, I can't seem to display that on the view.

Is there a special collection that I should bind the ASP.NET control in order to display the custom columns instead of the stock ones? What is the proper way to display a list view on an ASP.NET view Control?

A: Here's the code you can use to properly display the list view:

```
Private Function GetWeb() As Microsoft.SharePoint.SPWeb

    If Me._web Is Nothing Then

        Me._web =

Microsoft.SharePoint.WebControls.SPControl.GetContextWeb(My
Base.Context)

    End If

    Return Me._web

End Function
```

```
    Private Function GetList(ByVal listName As String) As
Microsoft.SharePoint.SPList

        Return Me.GetWeb().Lists(listName)

    End Function

    Private Sub BindViews()

        'BIND SINGLE PLAN INFORMATION

        Dim lstAirportInfo As Microsoft.SharePoint.SPList =
Me.GetList("Airports")

        Dim viewCol As
Microsoft.SharePoint.SPViewCollection =
lstAirportInfo.Views

        Dim view As Microsoft.SharePoint.SPView =
viewCol("All Items")

        Me.dvAirportInfo.DataSource = view.ViewFields

        Me.dvAirportInfo.DataBind()

    End Sub
```

Question 12: Extended Virtual Servers

I came across the term "extended virtual servers" in connection with Share Point portal server central administrator. What does that mean?

Is it to create multiple portals on single Share Point server, i.e., http://abc and http://xyz.etc?

A: You are right. Before you extend a virtual server, you must understand that it has nothing to do with Share Point. Once you extend it, Share Point will be configured to be used for that virtual website.

For example, you create a new virtual server xyz.com in your IIS, if you go into Share Point Central Administration, you will see it listed in the Virtual Server list, and you have the extend link there.

Once you click extend and then fill in the information for the AppPools etc. Share Point will "take over" that virtual server and configure it to run Share Point.

Question 13: Allowing Users To Read and Edit Their Own Issues

How can we allow users to only read and edit issues they created and have assigned to them? Or is there is a way that one group of users can read and edit only their own issues list items while another group is able to read and edit all?

Basically, I want to use it so the staff can send through jobs to the IT Department who would action them but I don't want users apart from the IT Department to be able to see other users' issues as some may be confidential.

A: You need only a certain person to view certain items and you could try to do this with views.

Example:

```
Make the default view where it is filtered by their Created
By = [Me]
And remove all other views.

Staff
- Only give permission to Add, View, Edit.

IT
- Give permission to Add, View, Edit, and manage views
- Have them create a PERSONAL view where they can see all
items.
```

In the end, the staff can only view their own items but IT will have the personal view and be able to see all items.

Question 14: Renaming a Company Web

I am running SBS 2003. I noticed that the default domain name that it uses is http://companyweb. However, I would like to rename it to a domain name that reflects our company name.

How do I accomplish this?

A: You can do the following:

In the DNS add a CNAME host record, e.g., mysharepoint.domain.com pointing to servername.domain.com. Then make sure you can ping the new name before changing anything else. Sometimes it takes a while for the DNS to be replicated.

Then in ISS, right click on the website where you have your company web and choose properties. In the website tab, click the "Advanced" button, mark the entry you will see in the list, and choose edit. In the host header value field, type in the new CNAME you added in the DNS (mysharepoint.domain.com).

Now you should be able to use that new name instead of just http://companyweb.

Note: Each site has their own virtual website. They all have the same IP address but respond to different host header names.

Question 15: Increasing the Size Limit

We like to use SPS/WSS in place of an FTP site. As a test user with contributor permissions, I tried to upload 54,000 KB zip file and got an error that it was too big.

How can I change this restriction?

A: The default upload size is set to 50mb.

To change this, do the following:

1. Go to the Portal Server Central Administration, Configure Virtual Server settings from the Virtual Server List page, and then click on the portal you want to modify.

2. Choose the option Virtual server general settings.

3. Then just change the setting to the "Maximum Upload Size."

Question 16: Share Point WSS in Windows Server 2003

Is there a visual safe source for document version control on a W2k server?

How much it will cost per user for a WSS license? Our Windows Server 2003 is a domain controller. I am not sure if it is a good idea to run WSS on this system.

After installing WSS on our Windows 2003 server, I have to add the user's username and password to access certain departmental websites created with WSS.

Will each user need to take one license for the server? The WSS users setup is within our WAN but do not have domain accounts, so I have to create using Active Directory account creation mode.

Since WSS is free for the Windows 2003 server, does this mean users added to access WSS websites don't need a license?

A: Windows Share Point Services is a part of the Windows 2003 license, so there are no additional costs for you to run WSS.

As long as this server is accessed by persons employed at your company, there's no need for any Windows Server External Connector licenses either. That is only needed if external resources (such as non-employees) are accessing Share Point.

You can install WSS on a domain controller.

If you use the internal access, you will need Win2003 Server CAL (Client Access License).

For use of external access (from internet or external non-employees) you need Win2003 Server External Connector licenses (which is a form of CAL licenses).

Question 17: Pictures On Share Point

I would like to add pictures of each employee on their profile page and I've already figured how to do this. The problem is I don't want to store all the pictures on the Share Point site because there's a lot and I'm afraid of the total size it will take up in the database.

Is there a way to link to these pictures from a network drive?

What other way is there apart from pointing to a URL?

A: Try using the format:

```
file:///<driveletter>:\<user>.jpg.
```

Question 18: Share Point Antivirus

We have trend server protect on our servers and trend's mail scanning running. I know there is a Trend Share Point Portal Protect but am not sure if it is a requirement or not.

With what appears to be just about everything covered with Trend Products, is there any possibility of a virus making it to my Share Point installation apart from viruses not detected by the current pattern files?

Is it possible for a virus to infect Share Point or is running Server protect on that server enough?

What does a portal antivirus product do that isn't already being done?

Does it really provide any protection to the server hosting the database but may stop macro type viruses in office documents from being spread to clients' access to those documents?

A: If you know that all your clients that are uploading documents to Share Point have a good antivirus protection on their machines, you might not need the Share Point Portal Protect.

Ordinary antivirus software running on the clients can't scan the documents that you have in Share Point since they are stored in the databases. What a Share Point specific antivirus system does is scan the databases and it can detect viruses in documents that are stored there.

Even if you have antivirus software that can scan database files I do not think you can detect any viruses in the share point databases, because the documents are stored as "blobs" in tables in the share point databases.

The Share Point antivirus software will go into the Share Point databases and scan the content there; it will not do any checks on files outside of Share Point.

However, one advantage of using antivirus software for Share Point will be the prevention of documents getting infected with a virus to uploaded /downloaded in/from share point.

Question 19: Saved File Storage

When I'm creating a new share document/list, where does it keep the files?

Is it still in the same place that I took it from or is it now in another place in the Share Point folder?

A: It is in the database; either WMSDE or SQL. Everything except the install files (and custom site definitions) are stored in the Database. The install files can be found here.

```
C:\Program Files\Common Files\Microsoft Shared\web server
extensions\60
```

And the file will only be at one location and that is the Database, WSS will make it look as if you where working with files and folders.

Question 20: Share Point and AutoCAD

Does AutoCAD work well in Share Point?

A: If you are just talking about adding AutoCAD files to Share Point, it is possible as long as the file extension is not on the blocked files list.

What might cause problems is when you want to choose to edit the document, I do not think Share Point will give you a choice by default to actually edit the file in AutoCAD. I would think you need to do some modification so you can choose to edit the documents in AutoCAD. Otherwise, the file will open up as read-only when you open it up in AutoCAD from the Share Point site.

You will need some kind of modification in the default program to be able to edit the file in AutoCAD.

Question 21: Searching Index in Share Point

How do I purge a search index in Share Point Service?

A: Do the following steps:

1. Go to Site Settings.

2. Configure Search and Index.

3. Manage Content Indexes and hover over the content index that you wish to purge.

4. Click "Reset Content Index" and your index will be purged.

Question 22: A New Portal

Why should I click on "Create Portal" if the Share Point is a Portal itself?

Do all these features like the WSS and web parts belong to the "portal" or to Share Point in general?

A: When you install Share Point Portal Server, you have to create a Portal. Installing SPS2003 does not automatically function as a portal.

You can host up to 15 portals in an installation.

So, basically, when the installation is done, you have all the requirements to start building Share Point Portals.

SPS2003 is built "on top" of WSS which is a requirement for SPS. When you have the SPS2003 installed, you will have both Portal and WSS functionality.

When it comes to the web parts you have some for WSS and some for SPS (keep in mind that SPS and WSS are two different products).

Question 23: Opening a New Pop-up Window

When we open Dispform.aspx of our list, we would like one of the fields/comments to open up in a new pop up window.

I know how to make the pop-up, but I don't know how to grab the data from the comments field. Is it possible to use JavaScript to grab data from this one field?

Below is my JavaScript to make the window pop up, but it doesn't capture the field.

```
<SCRIPT LANGUAGE="JavaScript">

<! -- Original:  Rick Johnson (frj11@ev1.net) -->

<! -- Web Site:  http://rickjohnson.tripod.com -->

<! -- This script and many more are available free online
at -->

<! -- The JavaScript Source!!
http://javascript.internet.com -->

<! - Begin

function popupWin() {

text =  "<html>\n<head>\n<title>Pop
Window</title>\n<body>\n";

text += "<center>\n<br>";

text += "Comments Text would go here";

text += "</center>\n</body>\n</html>\n";

setTimeout('windowProp(text)', 0);        // delay 0
seconds before opening

}

function windowProp(text) {
```

```
newWindow =
window.open('','newWin','width=340,height=250');

newWindow.document.write(text);

setTimeout('closeWin(newWindow)', 200000);    // delay 100
seconds before

closing

}

function closeWin(newWindow) {

newWindow.close();                // close small window and
depart

}

//  End -->

</script>
```

A: Just put a <div id="commentdiv"> around the Share Point lines you wanted to capture.

Then use this syntax to get the comment:

```
comment = document.getElementById("commentdiv").innerHTML
```

Question 24: Share Point Calendar Display

Whenever an event is added, it doesn't show the last day of the event in the calendar view. I added a vacation from Monday to Friday but in the calendar view, it only shows the "blocked off" days of Monday to Thursday. However, when I click the link, it shows the begin data as being Monday and the end date being Friday. It's the built in event list.

How can I make the changes display correctly in the calendar view?

A: When using the event list, the default time that is placed in "begin and end" is 12:00 a.m. Therefore, when an end day of the 2nd, the calendar will not highlight the 2nd because it thinks it ends first thing in the morning. You can either require the users to put a later date or built a custom list that only uses data and not time.

Changed the time from 12:00 a.m. to any other time and it will spread across the last day.

Question 25: Info Path and Exchange

We currently want to change our Outlook Forms to Info Path forms.

How can I make an Info Path form mimics an email with the "to: button" and all?

A: Info Path with SP1 can email forms. In the tools menu click submitting forms and you will have the option to email the form.

When the users finish the form and click submit, it will open the outlook where they will have the To: CC: etc.

Question 26: Oracle and Share Point

Is it possible for Share Point to pull data straight from an Oracle database and store the info on an SQL server?

A: You could always develop custom code to do what you want but direct access to you Share Point database is not supported and data can't just be copied. It needs to be in a specific format, so add the items to Share Point trough the object model.

Question 27: Hiding Fields In Custom Lists

I've created a custom list that contains an expiry field. The contents of which is calculated (today + 7) and which should be 'set-in-stone'.

Using a custom view, I've hidden the field in the list view, but when an item is selected from the list and the item detail view is displayed, the expiry field can be updated so that instead of expiring after 7 days, the item could remain indefinitely.

Is there a way of hiding or locking fields in the item detail view of a custom list?

A: If you are using a calculated data column with a default value, it will not be editable.

Make the type of the calculated column date/time and select only date.

The formula should be =Created+7; it's the date in the column created because calculated columns can't accept "Today" because it keeps calculating the value.

Question 28: Date Entry Format

When adding new items for events, announcements, etc. on my Share Point Installation, it specifies that dates be entered as M/D/YYYY:

Enter date in M/D/YYYY format.

Is it possible to change the date format to the day/month/year format?

A: Yes. You must change the locale. You should do this anyway because it also affects your time zone and the like.

In Share Point Portal Server you can do it with Site Settings -> Manage security and additional settings -> Modify regional settings.

In Share Point Services it Site Administration Pages -> Change regional settings.

Select the country that most of your users originate from, and you're finished.

Question 29: Adding URL To a "List" Through SDK

I have a "Links" list in which I want to insert a new link. I perform this operation through SDK and hope I can insert the new item but it does not work.

Here's some code I used:

```
//updating "Links" list...

//set URL field

this.addedItem["URL"] = this.currentSiteCollection.Url +
"/" +

this.urlTextBox.Text;

//set Country Name

this.addedItem["Country Name"] = this.titleTextBox.Text;

this.addedItem.Update();
```

As you can see I've created a new item that represents an URL to a new site created.

This is the result I get on my page:

```
"Country Name"

India

----> And on the same row... :)

"URL"

http://my_server/sites/home/"a_lot_of_subsites"/india
```

This URL is too big to see in a web page. Is there a way to set directly a URL description so I can see the description and not the full URL address?

A: Fill the URL property by a comma separated string:

```
itm["URL"] = "<URL>, <Description>";
```

For example:

```
itm["URL"] = "http://www.test.com, tekst to show";
```

Question 30: Share Point As a Web Server

We are using our Share Point Service as our normal web server. I am looking for some tips or hints for running multiple sites on IIS with Share Point.

Why is it that every time we type in the IP or "Name of the server" and view our Share Point site from our work stations, we need to pull up another site?

Where should we look so we can make some corrections?

A: Use host header forwarding in IIS when you run multiple sites or assign an additional IP address for the specific virtual website.

However, binding Share Point sites to an IP address might have some impacts when you want to do customization.

Create a host record in the DNS that point to the machine name, i.e., sharepoint.mycompany.com points to server name and in IIS, for the specific virtual server I have assigned host header forwarding to point to sharepoint.mycompany.com.

An alternative option is that if you are the Internet Information Service manager, you can do the following:

1. Select a virtual website or create one.

2. Go to its properties and under the Website Tab in the web site identification. Then you can use the IP address unassigned and use a different port number for each web server/site name.

3. Then go to advanced and select the item in the list of press edits to assign a host header.

Question 31: Search Function in WSS

Is there a search function in WSS for text and title of documents at any level of directory? If so, how does it work?

A: You could write your own web part and you could also alter the Stored Procedure in the database to search in "AND mode" and not "OR" as WSS does by default.

1. Go into SQL Enterprise Manager and open the stored procedure called

proc_FetchDocSearchResults (make a backup);

2. Add the following lines to the procedure before the line "SET

NOCOUNT ON":

DECLARE @CustSearchTerm nvarchar(255)

SET @CustSearchTerm = "" + @SearchTerm + ""

3. Find the word FreeTextTable and replace it with Contains Table

4. In the same line, change the variable @SearchTerm to @CustSearchTerm

Then a bit of code for the web part:

```
CODE:

SPSite mySiteCollection = new SPSite(servernaam);

SPWeb oRootSite = mySiteCollection.OpenWeb(<empty if you
search on top site

else "/subsite name>); //you can use this to go trough any
number of sites, just

make a loop.

PSearchResultCollection oSRSet =
oRootSite.SearchDocument(searchstring);

foreach( SPSearchResult oSR in oSRSet )

{

//oSR.Url //make output

//oSR.Title

}

Interface:

TextBox tb;

ImageButton btn_search;

LiteralControl lc;

protected override void CreateChildControls()

{

    tb=new TextBox();  //searchbox
```

```
tb.Width=180;

tb.Style["vertical-align"] ="3";

tb.MaxLength=255;

tb.CssClass="ms-searchbox";

Controls.Add(tb);

Controls.Add( new LiteralControl(" ") );

btn_search=new ImageButton();   //Zoek knop icon

btn_search.Style["vertical-align"] ="1";

btn_search.ImageUrl="_layouts/images/gosearch.gif";

Controls.Add(btn_search);

lc=new LiteralControl();

lc.Text="<br>";

Controls.Add(lc);
}
```

Then write something to compare the path of the search result with the scope you are looking in if you have a scope enabled search web part. I get the scope send to the web part from my navigation web part.

Question 32: Editing Contact Information

How can I edit contact information in the contact list section?

Under Documents and Lists and then Contact, the contact list does not have an option for editing each person's profile.

I have a Microsoft Share Point Product Technology book but it seem to be intended for Administrative functions only.

Is there another book or reference material that I can use?

A: If you have the proper user rights assigned (i.e., Contributor, etc.) and the contact list allows a contributor to edit items in the list, then it should be very easy for you.

Go into the Contact list and when you hover your pointer over the column that is linked to the edit menu, there you can choose to edit the user's information.

If you do not have any column that is linked to the edit menu, that can be changed by changing the view of the list. That is done by clicking modify settings and columns from the Action list on the left hand side once you are the Contact list.

In the Microsoft website you can easily find the Administrator guides and help section for both products. Just do searches on the MS website for administrator guide Share Point and you will find it.

Question 33: Problems with Custom List

I added a new field to the custom list (custlist) by adding the following entry to the schema.xml:

```
CODE:

<Field Type="Integer" Name="State" DisplayName="State"
Sealed="TRUE"

Hidden="TRUE" ReadOnly="FALSE"/>
```

I set hidden=true because I need this field completely hidden to the UI. But when I try to set or get the value in this field, I get an error (object reference not set to an instance of an object).

Here is the part of my source code:

```
CODE:

SPWeb myweb = SPControl.GetContextWeb(Context);

myweb.AllowUnsafeUpdates = true;

SPList list = myweb.Lists["List_name"];

list.Items[0]["State"] = 1; //an item with index 0 exits!!!

list.Items[0].Update();

output.Write(list.Items[0]["State"].ToString()); //this
statement causes the error
```

If I try this code with the "title" field of the custom list or if I set hidden=false then it works.

How do I get this to work?

A: CODE:

```
SPWeb myweb = SPControl.GetContextWeb(Context);
```

```
myweb.AllowUnsafeUpdates = true;

SPList list = myweb.Lists["List_name"];

SPListItem item = list.Items[0];

item.["State"] = 1;

item.Update();
```

Question 34: Change Main Site's Help Link

I've change the ONET.XML files' entire Help link from the default to my new, custom link. However, those changes didn't propagate to the main pages and the portal site itself.

The main site homepages still have:

```
javascript:HelpWindowKey("NavBarHelpHome")
```

The portal site still has:

```
http://portal/default.aspx#URL#
```

Is there any way to modify these?

A: Do an indexed search of all the .js, .aspx, .asp files on your portal server and find the key.

On your portal box, go to:

```
DRIVE: \Program Files\Common Files\Microsoft Shared\web
server

extensions\60\TEMPLATE\LAYOUTS\1033
```

In here, you'll find the OWS.JS; the magic file that contains, apparently, the very key and difficult to find JavaScript definitions for your entire portal.

In here, you will find several scripts for "help":

```
HelpWindowHelper
```

```
HelpWindowKey
```

```
HelpWindowUrl
```

```
HelpWindow
```

They appear to each build off of each other, starting with HelpWindowHelper that renders the initial URL.

So, change the code from:

```
CODE:
function HelpWindowHelper(strParam)

{

    var strHelpUrl;

    if (strParam == "")

        strHelpUrl = "/_layouts/" + L_Language_Text +
"/help.aspx" + "?LCID=" +

 L_Language_Text;

    Else

        strHelpUrl = "/_layouts/" + L_Language_Text +
"/help.aspx" + strParam +

"&LCID=" + L_Language_Text;

    var wndHelp = window.open(strHelpUrl, "STSHELP",

"width=270,height=500,menubar,scrollbars,toolbar,resizable"
);

    wndHelp.focus();

}
```

to:

```
CODE:

function HelpWindowHelper(strParam)

{

    var wndHelp =
window.open("http://wpsportal1/sites/wpsportalhelp/",

"STSHELP", "menubar,scrollbars,toolbar,resizable");

    wndHelp.focus();

}
```

Take investigatory information and force it to a specific URL.

This seems to fix both the Portal and the Sites. And everything is going to the customized Help site rather than the built in help.

Question 35: Document Library in Share Point 2003

Is there a way to tell a document library in Share Point 2003 to show file extensions?

We want the user to be able to look at the library and see "company.doc" instead of just "company."

A: There is no way to do this without modifying xml "configuration" files.

You can do it via FrontPage but that will only allow you to change the extension to show up in one view. And you have to convert the web part to an XSLT data view. If you want it to show up on all views, you have to modify the XML files manually.

I would not recommend doing this if you are not familiar with customization of Share Point because it is very easy to break a site.

Question 36: "Domain\Username" On Share Point Site

There are some user names that come up as "domain\username" and some that are just "username" on our Share Point site. We would like them all to be "username."

How do we go about making this change? It seems to apply to just a few users. Even if I delete the users and then recreate them, the username still appears as "domain\username."

We are using the Share Point Portal server. It seems that I can change the preferred name only in the main site. And that works. But it does not seem to apply to user accounts in team sites. When I go to manage users in team sites, I can't seem to change their preferred name.

A: If you are running Share Point Portal server check:

Site Settings -> manage Profile Database > View User Profiles.

There, you can set a preferred name and you can just make sure that the "username" is entered there.

If you are running Share Point services check:

Site settings -> View information about site users.

There you can click on the user you want to view/change information for. Then choose edit user information and you will be able to edit the display name of the user.

And under the team sites, you go to "view information about site users" and you can change the display name there.

Question 37: Saving Documents Locally

I am currently running Share Point Service and we are using it as a central document repository.

How can I stop the users from saving on their local PC's so that they will have the latest version that is available?

A: Well this is not a setting that you can do within Share Point. If a user has the right in Windows to save files locally, that will also be possible within Share Point.

What I have done on users here is that I have mapped their "My Documents" to a server, so that it is not placed locally on the user's computer. However, they can still save files onto the local drives such as the C: drive.

Question 38: Password For Document Libraries

I want to have several folders listed on one page for each employee. The employees will be saving their timesheets in these folders.

Is there any way to put a password on each folder so that each employee can only view their folder and add to it?

A: You can set permissions on Document Libraries and Lists not on folders or specific documents.

You have to create a separate Document Library for each employee and only set that specific user to be able to access the Document Library.

After you have created the Document Library, you can set the permissions on it by going into the library.

1. Click "modify settings and columns."

2. Choose change permissions for this Document Library and there you will have to remove all the site groups that were added by default and add only the user account for the users that will have access to the library.

However, if you choose to display the Document Libraries on the Quick Launch bar, all users that have access to the site will be able to see the Document Library, but only the user you granted access will be able to open it.

Question 39: Restrictions On File Sizes

Is there a way to restrict the size of documents allowed in a document library?

I want to upload documents that are 50 MB or less.

Is there a way to display file sizes in a document library so that users can see the sizes of the files before opening?

A: The default maximum size of files in Share Point is set to 50MB/file.

You can change this setting in the Central Administration for Share Point.

In the Central Administration, choose "configure virtual server settings" and choose your virtual server. Under Virtual Server Management, choose Virtual server general settings. There you will see "maximum upload file size" and by default it is set to 50MB.

You can also add file size as a display option in the "Edit View" area.

Question 40: View Site Usage Data

I am trying to view the site usage data for my Share Point 2003 server. I have enabled and configured it. On the team sites, I can see the data under "Management and Statistics," and "View site usage data." But on the main site, where I really want the data, I don't see any way to view it. There is no view option that I can find.

Is there a way I could re-configure the site so I have a "View Option" for the site usage data?

A: If you want to check usage statistics and access everything on the Site Administration page at the top most Portal site level, then all you need to do is:

Add "/_layouts/1033/webadmin.aspx" to the end of http://[your portal], or any other page under the main Portal site.

This is a part of Share Point that you cannot actually access via link from the main Portal site. There is no link to this actual administration page unless you create a new sub site and then there is a link for that particular sub site.

Question 41: Importing Information

Is it possible to import information into a Share Point list from an Excel spreadsheet?

A: Yes, it is possible. Go to Create, and under custom lists you have the option to import a spreadsheet. Basically, you create a custom list and choose which spreadsheet file to import.

You need an application compatible with Share Point services for this (e.g., Office 2003 Pro).

Question 42: Custom Search Form in Share Point Service 2003

I want to create a custom search form for a list in SPS2003 that allows searching of all items in the list based on wildcard matches, etc.

It should appear on top of the "All Items" view. I know users could use SP's built in search facility, but I want to restrict the output to the contents of the list only.

A: You will be creating a Custom Web Part Page, adding a Form Web Part, and your List Web Part, and then connecting them.

1) Create Web Part Page. Place it in a public Document Library labeled User "Full Page Vertical."

2) Open the Page, and Modify it. Add Web Part.

3) Find the Form Web Part, and then add it.

4) Find your List View Web Part, and add it below the Form web part.

5) From the Modify Menu, Open "Connections." This will be a wizard that will connect your form fields to the List View.

6) If you want more advanced forms, you need to edit the html directly in the form.

Question 43: Search Results Modification

I am using Share Point Portal Server 2003 and want some modifications to the search configuration.

I am trying to implement the suggestion that I found in this article regarding having search results show up in a new window. It states that you can add a tag "OpenNewWindowForMatchingItems" to have your links open in a new window.

Where can this tag actually be placed?

A: You have to use FrontPage to add the tag to the Actual Search Results Web Part. You can do it by modifying the DWP file. FrontPage will allow you to edit it directly.

Question 44: Uploading Access Database

When attempting to upload an Access database to a Share Point document library on Share Point 2003 and Windows 2003 on an Intranet, I get the message:

"Form Validation Error... The following file(s) have been blocked by the administrator: [my database]".

I created the database and haven't set any security on it. I tried changing my Internet Explorer security to low, and I tried with the database on my desktop rather than a network drive, without effect. How can I upload successfully?

A: Here's the solution:

1. Remove the File type from the "Blocked File Types." You will find it when logged on as an administrator.

2. Site Settings/Share Point Portal Server Central Administration/Blocked File types and remove it.

Question 45: Share Point Services Authentication

I've installed Windows Share Point Services 2.0 on my server. How can I authorize a consultant to log in to our Share Point site without being in our domain? It is only giving me the option to authenticate by domain\username.

I changed authentication method in IIS 6 to Basic Authentication. When I create a user, it states "USER DOES NOT EXIST." How do I create a user to log in with a simple username and password?

Do I also have to create a user account on the network for everyone that needs to log into WSS?

A: You can do the following:

1. Create a local user on your WSS server: user1.

2. Set your WSS site to basic authentication.

3. Navigate to your site.

4. Log in as someone that manages the WSS site.

5. Add the user by using servername\user1 and give him the rights needed to perform his job.

6. Log out.

7. Navigate again to your site.

8. In the "authorize dialog box" use servername\user1 and fill in the correct password that should work.

To answer your other question, yes, you have to create a user account on the network for every consultant.

If your server is a member of a domain, you can use domain accounts. E.g., domainname\useraccount.

Question 46: Access For Usage and Management

Does Share Point Server 2003 support https access for usage and management?

As KB831106 said, it didn't support SSL termination. Say if the SPS2003 server is behind firewall, and the firewall do 1-to-1 static Nat for the SPS, and opening port 443 for outside access mapped to Share Point Service, in this case will it work?

A: It can support SSL. Just install a certificate on the virtual server in IIS on which you run your portal on or only the administration website or both. It's just IIS configuration, you don't need to do anything within the portal.

Question 47: Share Point V2 Default Install Settings

I am currently running Server 2003 and Share Point Services V2 and everything seems to be working just fine. My problem is that I have my drive split into two separate partitions. One contains all the web sites being hosted on the machine, mail root, FTP sites, etc. The other one contains the OS and is a lot smaller.

When installing Share Point V2, by default it installs the software and MSDE on the system drive (C:) and does not give you the option of changing it. Thinking it was similar to Share Point V1 where all of the documents, files etc. for each site are saved in the website folder, I did not see drive space being a problem.

After looking at the configuration I noticed a big difference. With Share Point V2, all files saved to the site get saved somewhere else. Does it mean in my case it puts it on my system drive? This creates a huge problem for us considering that my system drive was partitioned to a size big enough for the OS and some breathing room.

Is there any way to reconfigure the setup and the placement of the database? Or is there a way to do a custom install to be able to specify where it gets installed?

A: If you install the SQL client tools packaged with SQL 2000, you will get the Enterprise Manager console which allows you to connect to any SQL-based server (including MSDE) and perform all the normal SQL admin functions from a GUI interface.

You can reconfigure all your Share Point settings using a plethora of confusing parameters for the command-line utility stsadm.exe, but Enterprise Manager works much better. When you register your server in Enterprise Manager, be sure to use MachineName\Sharepoint for the server instance, rather than just the MachineName. Once you've got it registered, you can see all your Share Point databases and move their data file locations to a happier partition.

Question 48: Share Point Portal 2001

I'm using the Share Point Portal 2001 Evaluation edition. I have copied a sample 200 files to the "Documents" folder in the Share Point web and they are all contract word document. Each file is named "TT1234" where 1234 is the reference number.

If I ask the Share Point web to Index and update, I cannot search under these references until I type in the document title, description and keywords manually.

Will this work if I move all of my existing documents into the "Documents" folder which is in the portal?

A: You may need to run a full update on your content sources. Try this on the Share Point server:

Open up Windows Explorer, go to Network Neighborhood.

Go to the http://<your workspace> at <your server name>.

Go to Management folder and click on Content Sources.

Under Content sources, right click on your workspace and select Start full update.

After the full update, then, yes, this will work for the complete workspace. You can add all sorts of documents (be it word, excel, PPT, etc.) and the above procedure will include everything in the indexing of search, no matter where it is in the workspace.

Note: You can put a load of documents in the "Documents" folder and tell the portal to do a Full Update and it will automatically categorize/index everything in the folder.

Question 49: Back-up Share Point With STS Admin

I want to backup Share Point with STS Admin to a file located on the local drive and then our backup product to back that file up offsite.

How can I run the script daily, replacing the old backup file?

Where can I get a script/batch file to use for backing up Share Point?

Are there issues running the STS Admin during business hours?

A: To create a script that backup your sites using stsadm.exe is a very simple task. If you have one virtual website, then you just need one line which is the actual command line with backup parameter for STS Admin. Put it in a batch file and run it as a scheduled task. Instructions on how to use the STS Admin tool is described in The Administrators Guide.

Below is a procedure which details how I have done it for backing up all my virtual websites. I have 50 of them so I just made a simple script.

I created two script files and one text file.

The text file is named: sites.txt.

It contains two columns: one is the address to the site without http, like this:

"sharepointsite.com"

The second column contains the name I want for the backup file, like this:

"sharepointsite.dat"

The first script file I named: "backup.cmd"

It contains:

```
"DATE /T > BACKUP.log

FOR /F "TOKENS=1,2" %%i IN (sites.txt) DO CALL
BACKUP_SITES.CMD %%i %%j"
```

The second file is named: "BACKUP_SITES.CMD"

It contains the following:

```
@echo off

echo Start %1 >> backup.log

Time /T >> backup.log

call "C:\Program Files\Common Files\Microsoft Shared\web
server

extensions\60\BIN\STSADM.exe" -o backup -url "http://%1" -
filename

d:\backup\%2.dat -overwrite
```

```
echo Stop %1 >> backup.log

Time /T >> backup.log
```

I run my backup jobs outside of business hours just to make sure it does not affect performance. It depends on how much data and how many sites you are backing up and also how many concurrent users you have using the sites.

I would recommend you to do the backups on non-office hours, just to make sure that you do not have any problems in getting all the data backed up properly.

Question 50: Dropdown List

I have created a web part for Share Point using asp.net 2.0. I have the code to create a textbox in the edit zone and it work but I need it to be a dropdown list.

How can I resolve this?

```
using System.Collections.Generic;

using System.Text;

using System.Web;

using System.Web.UI;

using System.Web.UI.WebControls;

using System.Web.UI.WebControls.WebParts;

namespace WebPartV3

{

    public class Pyr : WebPart

    {
```

```
private string _Pyr;

[

WebBrowsable(true),

Personalizable(PersonalizationScope.Shared),

WebDisplayName("Pyr"),

WebDescription("Chose your information"),

]

public string GetSetPyr

{
    Set

    {
        _Pyr = value;

    }

    Get

    {

        return _Pyr;

    }

}

protected override void CreateChildControls()

{

    if (_Pyr == "" || _Pyr == null)

    {

        _Pyr = "blank.ascx";

    }

    Control Pyr =
this.Page.LoadControl(@"/controls/" + _Pyr);

    this.Controls.Add(Pyr);

}
```

```
    }

}
```

A: Do the following:

```
namespace PyrWebPartV3
{
    public class Pyra : WebPart
    {
        string _PyrUC;
        public enum enumSample
        {
            Pyr = 0,
            Pyr1 = 1,
            Pyr2 = 2,
        };

        private enumSample _Pyr;
        [
        WebBrowsable(true),
        Personalizable(PersonalizationScope.Shared),
        WebDisplayName("Pyr"),
        WebDescription("Choose your information"),
        ]

        public enumSample GetSetPyr
        {
            Set
            {
                _Pyr = value;
            }
            Get
            {
                return _Pyr;
            }
        }

        protected override void CreateChildControls()
        {
            if ((int)_Pyr == 0)
            {
                _PyrUC = "blank.ascx";
            }
            else if ((int)_Pyr == 1)
            {
                _Pyr = "pyr2_all.ascx";
            }
            else if ((int)_Pyr == 2)
            {
                _PyrUC = "pyr2_1.ascx";
```

```
        }

        Else
        {
            _PyrUC = "blank.ascx";
        }

        Control Pyr =
this.Page.LoadControl(@"/controls/" + _PyrUC);

        this.Controls.Add(Pyr);
    }
  }
}
```

Question 51: Modifying a Metadata

While programmatically uploading file to the document library, I need to set my own title and description properties for that particular file.

How can we modify metadata for file in a document library?

A: Use the File. Add the method of the SPFolder class:

```
//Get the folder that should store the document
SPFolder folder = web.Folders["Library3"];
folder.Files.Add(
);
```

Question 52: Deploying a VB.net Solution

How can I deploy a VB.net web page on Windows 2003 Server using that Page Viewer web part that is also running in Share Point Services?

The server is running IIS, and has .net framework 2.0 installed. But when I copy over the program directory and files, I was not able to run the program. I keep getting an error that the page is not found.

How do I make this work?

A: You need to "exclude" the path of the ASP.Net application using Share Point Central Administration.

Question 53: Share Point Portal Search Services Is Not Working

How can I resolve some issues regarding Share Point Portal Search services that are not working?

A: Share Point Services needs to crawl in order to update the search and index database with metadata. In order for this to happen, the server performing the crawling needs to have proper access to crawl. If it doesn't, it will not be able to find any data.

Due to some recent Microsoft updates, there is one tip to try that may solve some issues. On the server, within the browser settings do the following:

```
Tools --> Internet Options --> Connections Tab --> LAN
Settings button;
```

Check to see if the automatically detect settings box is checked.

If the client browser on the server cannot access Internet content, then there is nothing to crawl. This may fix the issue.

Question 54: Share Point Portal Server 2003 Custom ASPX-pages

I made a custom ASPX page (details.aspx) that's going to be referred by a Hyperlink Column from within a Web Part:

```
newColumn_Companyname.DataNavigateUrlFormatString
="javascript:void

window.open('details.aspx?contact_id={0}', null,'left=1;
top=500; width=1024;

height=150; scrollbars=1; resizable=0')";
```

The new Internet Explorer window was opened. I only get a "404 page cannot be found" error.

Where do I have to put my custom made ASPX page to make it work?

A: If the ASPX page is a web part page, then it can be put in a document library.

If it is an ASP.Net application, you should create a managed path and place the file there.

Question 55: Share Point Services and SQL Server 2000

I got Share Point Services and am working with SQL Server 2000 on my development web server. But my other sites on that server are all failing with "Page cannot be found." If I uninstall Share Point, they start working again.

It seems like Share Point is controlling something about the security, but I cannot figure out what it's doing.

How do I fix this?

A: Do the following:

1. Go to Administrative tools.

2. Share Point Central Administration.

3. Extend or Upgrade Virtual Server.

4. Define managed Paths.

5. Add a new path.

6. Include the path of the other site and press Ok.

Question 56: WSS Evaluation Questions

WSS Security:

a) Are users assumed to be "managed clients" under Active Directory?

b) Is there a Forgot Password feature?

c) Can users "Self Register" themselves?

d) Are Sites or pages and its Web Part allowed security role based access assignment?

I need to create a Portal that contains documents and discussions in a "chain of command" hierarchy. Where a CEO can access/view all content, VP Marketing can only access/view content under their respective department. Users under this department can access/view only their content.

Is WSS the right product for this type of portal, considering its security/role structure?

A: The answers are given in the order they were asked:

a) WSS can be installed in Account Creation mode that allows WSS to control the accounts. The Default is Domain Account Mode where accounts must exist and be created by administrators.

b) No, but I wrote one.

c) No. In Account Creation Mode, site owners can create accounts. A site owner does not need special network privileges.

d) Yes, there is role-based access control. I recommend reviewing the TechNet page on Managing Site Groups and Permissions.

Question 57: Accessing Share Point Document Library

I am developing one asp.net web site. I have to use Windows Share Point Services (WSS) as document repository and create one site in WSS.

In that site, I have to create one document library. I want to upload the document to that WSS site's document, downloading the documents from WSS site's document library, version control of documents, check in and check-out of documents. All this I want to do from my Asp.Net web site.

How can I accomplish my objectives?

A: There are four methods you can use:

1. Share Point object model

2. Share Point web services

3. WEBDAV

4. FPRPC

The FPRPC is the most suitable for that. You can get a sample application on FPRPC to do that on www.gotdotnet.com. The application's name is Share Pad.

Question 58: Portal Server and Share Point Services

I am doing an application that will watch a particular directory/folder (FileSystemWatcher) and upload the files and folder that are added or modified in that directory to the Share Point Service.

This I did as a windows services application. In my application I had used Share Point File, Share Point Folder, etc. classes.

I want to install my application into a system. I was wondering whether that system should contain the Portal Server to be installed or is the share point server alone enough for that?

A: You only need the core Windows and Share Point Services (WSS) and not the Portal Server.

Question 59: Forms and Share Point

I have a form that was created in HTML and uses the Form method="post" action="mailto:name@host.com.

It works every time on my UNIX web server. I uploaded it into Share Point form and now when I fill it out and submit, nothing happens even if I already added an SMTP relay in Share Point.

How can I resolve this issue?

A: Share Point runs on top of ASP.Net and uses its post back feature which uses a form. Your form is nested inside the main form.

1. You have to create a new Web Part page.

2. Add a Page Viewer Web Part to the page.

3. Configure the part to display at your HTML page.

4. The result will be an IFRAME and your form should work correctly.

Question 60: Default Database Location

How can I have Share Point Portal installed on a minimum of 2 servers which is Share Point Services (Front-end Web, search) and Database (Configuration, SITE, PROF, SERV), job and index wherever it fits best?

A: While installing the Database in the proper place, the first time is to make sure the Database Server default install path is set to wherever you want the Database files created.

While moving the database, it is always better to do it right the first time.

The DBA should have set this already, but just in case it isn't set, or if there is a different place you'd like the database installed, change it on the database server first prior to installation. This will make sure that Share Point Service creates the database in the proper place the first time.

Question 61: Uploading Word Document From a Client Machine

I am doing an application that will watch a particular directory/folder (FileSystemWatcher) and upload the files and folder that are added or modified in that directory to the Share Point server.

When the word document in the client machine is opened, it is still saved in the watching directory. The file is not uploaded to the server.

Sometimes it takes ~$test.doc as the filename. Even if got the filename test.doc as correctly, the server returns an error "The file is used by another process."

What seems to be the problem?

A: Your problem is when the word is opened, a file with ~$ as prefix will be created and also you can't access the file when the file is opened.

You have to use the file share property while reading the content of the file to overcome this problem.

Question 62: Deleting Subfolders

I am doing an application that will watch a particular directory/folder (FileSystemWatcher) and upload the files and folder that are added or modified in that directory to the share point server.

I want to delete a subfolder in the Share Point Service.

```
Dim docLibPath As String =
ConfigurationSettings.AppSettings("DocUploadPath")

Dim thisProjectWeb As SPWeb =
SPControl.GetContextWeb(context)

thisProjectWeb.AllowUnsafeUpdates = True

Dim parentfolder As SPFolder =
thisProjectWeb.GetFolder(docLibPath)

oldfolder = parentfolder.SubFolders(oldfoldername)

parentfolder.SubFolders.Delete(oldfolder.url)
```

It works fine if the oldfoldername=Firstfolder and returns error if the firstfolder

Contains any subfolder:

If oldfoldername=firstfolder/secondfolder.

How can I make this work?

A: Change the code as:

```
Dim docLibPath As String =
ConfigurationSettings.AppSettings("DocUploadPath")

Dim thisProjectWeb As SPWeb =
SPControl.GetContextWeb(context)

thisProjectWeb.AllowUnsafeUpdates = True
```

```
Dim parentfolder As SPFolder =
thisProjectWeb.GetFolder(docLibPath)

oldfolder = parentfolder.SubFolders(oldfoldername)

oldfolder.parentfolder.SubFolders.Delete(oldfolder.url)
```

Question 63: Developing Share Point Web Parts in XP

I don't have Share Point on my XP Pro dev station, and get namespace errors when trying to reference Share Point assemblies, for example, using Microsoft Share Point.

So how do I develop Share Point on XP? Must we develop on a W2003 server?

```
Env:
VS2005

Server :
W2003, WSS2.sp2, SPS2.sp2
```

A: You can copy the Microsoft Share Point assemblies from the server to your dev machine. When setting the reference, set Copy to Local = False. There is no need to have them with your assembly since they are already on the server.

Or, you can also install Visual Studio on a server machine.

Question 64: Document Library in WSS

I am trying to lay a breadcrumb trial for a Document Library in a WSS Team site.

How can this be done?

I know that we can do that at the site level, but how to get it done at the document library level?

The trial should be displayed like this:

```
TestSite Home > Documents and Lists > Misc Docs & >

New Folder > New Folder . . . and so on as the user
advances to the next sub folder.
```

A: This will certainly require a custom web part. It will require changes to the site template to include this web part in the document library form pages (AllItems.aspx, EditForm.aspx, DispForm.aspx).

There are some third-party breadcrumb web parts on the internet. I don't think any of them go down to the document library level, so there is some additional work to be done.

Question 65: Setting the Administration Page Access

When I try to make a new portal site, it gives me a successful creation of the portal. But when I click to browse and get to the next step, a dialog box appears for User Name and Password. And when I insert the user name and password, it gives me an authorized access.

How can I solve this and how can I set the administration page access that throws the IIS to throw the Share Point Service administration tools pages?

How can I do the right configuration for my basic portal?

A: Check your authentication methods in IIS. Integrated Windows authentication will prompt you for the username and password. You can enable anonymous access and go into site settings and set up whatever users you want to use the portal and switch it back to integrated windows authentication.

Question 66: Creating SSO Database On SSO Manage Portal

In my DC Server, I installed Share Point 2003 and I want to use SSO.

On SSO manage portal page, I filled user accounts for SSO and Enterprise application then clicked the ok button. It said: "fail to connect database server, after check your rights, try again."

I know installing Share Point 2003 needs some accounts or groups which belong to some powerful group. I created a user which belongs to local domain administrators and via the user to start SSO service and set IIS.

How can I address this issue?

A: It's the Share Point 1 of Windows 2003 that causes the problem.

The manage page is used to create SSO database and some tables.

The procedure can be done manually.

Running SQL query analyzer and opening the SSO created SQL script, sometimes in the program files\common shared\Microsoft SSO \SSO_schema.sql. Execute the script.

Then on manage portal page, just click the ok button.

Some alert message will appear, omit it and you will that find it's ok.

Question 67: Indexing PDF Files Content

How to use Share Point indexing the PDF file content from database?

The PDF file's content is stored as binary in Database.

A: Install the Adobe iFilter for PDF on the SQL Server machine.

Then, start a Full Population on the full-text index.

Question 68: Using Data Views

How do you use data views in FrontPage 2003?

A: Microsoft Windows Share Point Services, which is built on the Microsoft .NET Framework provides the component-based platform required for FrontPage data-driven functionality.

To create or edit a data-driven Web site using FrontPage 2003, your web site must be hosted on a server running Windows Share Point Services.

When you create a data-driven web site in FrontPage 2003, you add Data Views known also as Data View Web Parts. To your web site, to display data from data sources by using Extensible Style sheet Language Transformation (XSLT): a file that is used to transform XML documents into other types of documents, such as HTML or XML.

It is designed for use as part of XSLT. You can add Data Views that extract data from a variety of available data sources, such as Extensible Markup Language (XML) (Extensible Markup Language (XML): A condensed form of Standard Generalized Markup Language (SGML) that enables developers to create customized tags that offer flexibility in organizing and presenting information) files, Web services, Share Point lists, and OLE DB (OLE DB: A component database architecture that implements efficient network and internet access to many types of data sources, including relational data, mail files, flat files, and spreadsheets, compliant databases such as SQL Server, DB2, and Oracle.

You can customize Data Views to create custom displays of your data in WYSIWYG (WYSIWYG: an acronym for "What You See Is What You Get"). It allows you to view a document as it will appear in the final product and to directly edit the text, graphics, and other elements within that view format by using the Formatting toolbar.

You can create even more advanced customizations by using the Data View Details task pane, which includes the following:

Style: Choose a formatting style from a gallery of redesigned list view styles. You can also add a toolbar for site visitors to perform custom filtering on the list.

Filter: Specify criteria to display a subset of the data in the Data View.

Sort and Group: Display items in a particular order and optionally group them on a web page beneath collapsible headings.

Conditional Formatting: Set conditions for the data in your Data View.

Adding a Data View.

In Page view, at the bottom of the document window, click Design.

On the Data menu, click Insert Data View.

In the Data Source Catalog task pane, under the heading you want, click a data source. If the heading is collapsed, click to expand it.

Place your pointer over the data source you want, and then click the arrow next to it.

On the shortcut menu, click Insert Data View.

In the Data View Details task pane, set the properties you want.

Question 69: Adding Data Grid To a Web Part

I am having problems getting my data grid to work in this web part. Share Point comes up with a standard error saying there is something wrong with the web part. If I take the data grid out and if I use this code in a Web Form it works fine, but not in my web part.

```
protected DataGrid eventsDataGrid;

protected Label titleLabel;

protected DataSet dsEvents;

protected override void RenderWebPart(HtmlTextWriter
output)

{

this.Controls.Clear();

titleLabel.RenderControl(output);

output.WriteLine("<BR>");

eventsDataGrid.RenderControl(output);

}

protected override void CreateChildControls()

{

titleLabel = new Label();

titleLabel.Text = "Welcome";

Controls.Add(titleLabel);

string connectString =

"server=database;Trusted_Connection=true;database=databasen
ame;Min Pool

Size=1;Max Pool Size=1;Pooling=true;Connection Timeout=10";
```

```
dsEvents = SqlHelper.ExecuteDataset(connectString,
"StoredProcName");

eventsDataGrid = new DataGrid();

eventsDataGrid.DataSource = dsEvents.Tables[0];

eventsDataGrid.DataBind();

Controls.Add(eventsDataGrid);

}
```

A: Looking at your code, the potential error is in your last line of code.

```
Controls.Add(eventsDataGrid);
```

Try to place this line before calling the "DataBind()" method.
When you call this method, the grid will begin generating its own child control and without first been added to the proper naming container like the web part, the IDs of those child controls will be out-of-context.

Question 70: Running a Portal Site On Share Point

When I try to create a new portal site on Share Point I get this error:

```
Share Point Portal Server has detected Share Point Team
Services or FrontPage Server Extensions 2002 on this
virtual server and cannot extend a virtual server over
existing data. To proceed, migrate your data if necessary
and uninstall Share Point Team Services or FrontPage Server
Extensions 2002 from this virtual server.
```

So I prohibited FrontPage Server Extensions, but that didn't make the error go away.

In the Share Point Portal Server Central Administration, when I view the Virtual Server List:

```
Name                                    URL
Version
Default Web Site
http://[myservername]                   5.0.2.5012
Upgrade
```

If I click on Default Web Site, I get a help window "Upgrade a server or virtual server." I tried to do what it said in the help file, but then I ran into a different issue:

```
"Cannot upgrade virtual server http://[myservername]/.
Windows Share Point Services does not support in-place
upgrading of Share Point Team Services v.1.0 from Microsoft
or FrontPage Server Extensions. You have to migrate the
content from this virtual server to a new virtual server
extended with Windows Share Point Services."
```

What does all this mean? What do I need to do to get this portal up and running?

A: You have to look at the Installation guide before installing Share Point.

Some of the basic pre-system requirements are listed below:

1) Windows 2003 Server

2) Do not install FrontPage Server Extensions

3) Install ASP.NET

Question 71: Making an Event Work

I declared an event in a web part page for a button click. When I place the web part in a web page (aspx), the event is not triggering and it is working when I place it in a sub area of Share Point.

How do I make the event work?

A: If you are trying to handle a click that occurs inside a web part, then the handler must be declared inside the Web Part assembly.

For example, the following would be in the CreateChildControls routine:

```
Dim saveBtn as Button = New Button

saveBtn.ID = "save"

saveBtn.Text = "Save"

AddHandler saveBtn.Click, AddressOf SaveButton_OnClick

Controls.Add(saveBtn)
```

And the handler needs to be defined with the usual signature:

```
Public Sub SaveButton_OnClick(ByVal sender As Object, ByVal e As EventArgs)
```

Question 72: 800 x 600 Screen Resolution With Portals

We have a project where all the clients will be using 800x600 screen resolution and we are trying to decide which portal to use.

Will Share Point Portal Server 2003 function perform fine when the screen resolution is only 800x600?

A: SPS or WSS will perform fine under these conditions. Share Point was able to design different applications of different types and sizes.

There are few things on a Share Point page that are not percentage based or ratio based. You'll find the base portal shrinks and resizes beautifully.

Remember that your customizations to the portal are true no matter what you may use.

Question 73: Running Server Side Code On a Share Point Page

We have a few ASPX pages that I want to move into a WSS system.

I created a new and blank page on WSS site, and then opened the page in FrontPage 2003. I tried to add the code from the original page. All the web elements went right, but the Page_Load and other sub and functions gives me an error stating:

"The page contains server script, which is not supported on this server."

Is there any way to get this to work, or do I have to create a new customized web part for this?

A: A good way to host .ASPX pages in Share Point is to use the Page Web Viewer web part.

If you have .ASPX pages, you should run them in a path which is not managed by WSS. The reason for this is that WSS uses its own ISAPI DLL to parse the incoming pages, although this is very similar to ASP.NET it is not the same.

If you put your pages on the server and set the folder they are located in as an unmanaged path, the Share Point ISAPI DLL will not try to interpret those pages and they will be left to the ASP.NET.

Another option is to make this part of the template that Share Point site is based on. Now I'm not sure how complex you can get in that ASPX page, but I just thought you might want to be aware of this as an option. Especially if you want that page to be a part of a template as different sites are created.

Question 74: Dial-up Connection

Does Share Point Portal 2003 typically perform well over a dial up connection?

A: The answer really depends on how much bandwidth your users need. If they will be uploading and/or downloading huge documents, it might not work so well. If they just want to view the data, then it should work reasonably well considering it is a dial up.

Question 75: Determining Bottleneck's Performance

We're getting a timeout on a query that uses a standard web part but does a lot of formatting of the results.

I adjusted the timeout setting in web.config from 7 seconds to 70 seconds and now the query will complete but it takes a long time.

I would like to analyze why the page/query is slow. For example, determine whether the web server or the back-end database server is the limiting factor so I can consider upgrading the right resource to improve the performance.

How can I determine where the performance bottleneck is?

A: You can do some simple test in order to determine the bottleneck in such a situation. Try the following:

1. Run the query through Query Analyzer and see how long it takes to return that data. If it takes five minutes, you know that's the problem. If it comes back instantly you know it's not.

2. The problem can also be bandwidth which deals with the size of the data going across the network. If you are sending your page Megs of data, it will take time to download.

3. Another thing to check is the CPU Usage on the web server. If it goes up a lot when you load the web part, then it is the formatting of the results.

Question 76: Portal Server and Public Websites

A company has a small business server with Share Point services. They are running a Share Point based intranet, and possible project sites.

Is it possible to have a public website on the same server which is also running from portal server that uses parts of the same information and data published on the intranet and project sites?

Is this a good solution to share information/news etc.?

A: Yes. Share Point is a good solution for your situation. The web site can be set to an anonymous logon, and you control the access rights for that user very tightly, it can even be very secure.

The good part of it also is that WSS is free.

Question 77: WMSDE and SQL Server

Can WMSDE and SQL Server 2000 co-exist on the same server?

If yes, how can we find out whether Share Point Services installed on the same server is using WMSDE or SQL Server 2000?

A: They can coexist on the same server. To see which SQL Instance that your WSS is using, you can go to the "Manage Content Database Settings" in the Share Point Central Administration Tool.

Question 78: Single List Documents From Multiple Libraries

I'm trying to use WSSV2 as a combination of collaboration and document management tool. Contributors access and update documents. Readers see and print from their browsers.

Is there an easy way to link a single instance of a document to multiple library access points and list documents from multiple libraries in a single list?

Here are a couple of examples.

Example 1:

A corporate procedure is available to contributors for access and editing from a library based on regulatory relationships. The same document is available to read/print on the company intranet based on topic for employee reference.

Example 2:

A group of documents from different libraries is required to complete a task.

The document owners each have their own library for the documents they control. The end user needs to access the current version of several documents from various libraries at a single location.

A: Do the following steps:

1. Create a Word document listing the various documents needed to perform the required task.

2. In Word, add a hyperlink to a document title.

3. Switch to WSS. Right click the document link you want to open.

4. Select "Properties."

5. Left click the URL in the dialog box.

6. Do a "Ctrl A" to select the URL.

7. Do a "Ctrl C" to copy the URL.

8. Switch back to the Word document.

9. Do a "Ctrl V" to paste the URL into the dialog box and Save.

For some reason you have to use the "Ctrl X" option since cut, copy, and paste will not work. Do not close the dialog box in WSS until after you "Ctrl V" the URL into the Word box or you get a link to the temporary directory.

You also have to go back and "find and replace" the server alias with the FQDN due to inter-company network bridges.

Next is creating either a separate document library for the Word "containers" or set up a separate site to keep the users completely away from the owners.

Question 79: SQL Connection in Web Part

I need to make a connection to SQL Server on another server. The connection works fine as an ASPX page outside of Share Point, but when I try the same code in a web part inside of Share Point it has no connection. This database is outside the content databases that are created when you install Share Point services.

This is the connection string:

```
cn.ConnectionString = "User ID=a;Password=b;Persist
Security Info=False;Initial
Catalog=MasterContacts;Data Source=MySqlServer;"
```

Is this a permission issue? Do I need to change a setting in a Share Point configuration file?

A: This may be a connection issue. When you run the code inside of Share Point, you must provide the user identity of the Application Pool running your Share Point Web Site, permission to connect to the database. When your web part is running under Share Point, all access rights that are required for the web part should be granted to this user.

Question 80: Different Views To the Navigation Menu

I'm working on a custom navigation Web Part. If the user is inside a List page, i.e., a Document Library, I want the navigation menu to show the different Views of this particular list.

How do I accomplish this?

Am I on the right track if I have to use the View Selector class?

A: The Share Point List object has a Views property that returns the List's View Collection. You can do it from there.

Question 81: Creating Back-up of a Document

We have an extensive document library that gets backed up nightly but we have run into a situation and would like to avoid it again in the future.

We would like a way to avoid losing important documents accidentally by somehow creating/updating a copy on a different server each time the document is checked in.

Is there a way to create a back-up of a document when a user checks it in?

A: If you turn on document versioning in Share Point, each time the document is checked in, Share Point will automatically create a new version and save the old one.

Click on "Documents and Lists," click on the document library name, and then click on "General Settings" and change "Document Versions" to "YES."

Question 82: Document Management Tool

Are Share Point services good for document management?

If not what tools/software are good for it?

A: Share Point is not really a Document Management tool, but more of a collaboration tool. You can look at such products as Documentum, Hummingbird, and FileNet which have hefty price tags, but have advanced document management functionality.

Question 83: Navigate Back To Portal Homepage

How do I navigate back to the main portal from My Site?

A: To navigate from your My Site back to the Portal Home do the following:

1. Click My Links in the top right navigation bar.

2. Click My Share Points.

3. Click Home.

This will get you back to your Portal Homepage.

Question 84: Customize and Extend Share Point Task

Is it possible to extend and customize Share Point Task lists for specific requirements?

A: One great feature of Share Point is the ability to extend and customize the built in List types (such as Announcements, Contacts, Issues and Tasks) to meet your requirements.

The Credit Control department is responsible for reviewing the financial details of the company's suppliers and customers, setting and reviewing credit agreements, and enforcing credit control. They currently use a standard Share Point Task List to allocate and control work to the departments Credit Analysts.

Question 85: Displaying User's Name

How to display the name of the logged on user?

A: This "how to" will walk you through creating a web part that will display the current logged on user.

1. Create a new Announcements list and name it Logged on As.

2. Edit the "All Items view" and only have the "Title" being displayed.

3. Add a new item filling out only the title field. This could simply be your name or some general text. We recommend keeping it to one word for simplicity's sake.

4. Open the site in FrontPage and open the default.aspx page.

5. Insert a Data View Web Part based on the newly created Announcements (Logged On As) list.

6. In the data view properties window, click Conditional Formatting.

7. Remove the header columns (Title, Modified, etc.).

8. Remove the Modified date and any other data fields except for Title.

9. Select the "new Title" data value and Click on Create.

10. Click on Show Content.

11. Create a Condition that says: Title EQUALS [Current User] and click OK back to the Design view.

12. Type "Welcome:" next to the Title data value.

13. Switch to Code view.

Find the following code:

```
<td class="ms-vb"><xsl:if test="normalize-space(@Title) =
$UserID"><span><xsl:value-of
select="@Title"/></span></xsl:if></td>
```

Change this code to this:

```
 <td class="ms-vb"><xsl:if test="normalize-space(@Title) =
$UserID"><span><xsl:value-of
select="@Title"/></span></xsl:if>Welcome:
<xsl:value-of select="$UserID"/></td>
```

14. Save the page.

15. Browse to the page and login.

Note: When using this code, the conditional statement has to run before the data can be viewed otherwise no Username will be displayed. Feel free to change the "welcome:" to any such text you want.

Question 86: Enhancing the Toolbar

How do you enhance the usability of the Toolbar using a web part?

A: To enhance the usability, look, and feel of your Share Point pages you can add the Page Toolbar web part to your pages. The toolbar will add a number of common features to your page quickly and easily.

Question 87: Hiding Site Templates

How do you hide site templates when creating new sites?

A: This "how to" will explain hiding the default templates from the list of site templates when creating new sites. This works on both Share Point Portal Server 2003 and Windows Share Point Services.

1. Browse to \Program Files\Common Files\Microsoft Shared\Web Server Extensions\60\Template\60
This directory is where all the templates are managed.

2. Click the XML sub folder.

3. Open WebTemp.XML
To hide the site template from the gallery simply change Hidden="FALSE" to Hidden="TRUE"

4. Finally do an IISRESET and try to create another verifying that the hidden sites are actually hidden!

Question 88: Search Box in Windows Share Point

How do you add a search box in Windows Share Point Services?

A: This "How To" will explain adding a search box to a page that doesn't have one, or if you want you can add this to the page itself instead of the default position.

1. Open your site in FrontPage 2003.

2. Open default.aspx.

3. Copy this line of code:

```
<SharePoint:ViewSearchForm ID="L_SearchView" Prompt="Search
this site"

Go="Go" Action="searchresults.aspx" runat="server"/>
```

4. Paste it into a new site or new page.
Search as a test.

Question 89: Hiding Items in "Create" Button

How do you hide items under the "Create" button?

A: This "how to" will cover hiding certain items under the Create button in Windows Share Point Services. This may come in handy to wrap some governance around what can be created within team sites.

1. Within the Share Point File system [drive letter: \\program files\common files\Microsoft shared\web server extensions\60\template\1033\sts\xml] edit the ONET.XML file.

2. Search for the word "Forms." It will bring you to the LISTEMPLATE that handles the information for the Forms Library.

3. Comment out the section that should be hidden.

4. Use <! -- CODE --> to comment items out.

5. Run an IISRESET.

6. REFRESH the site in a browser. The Forms Library will disappear.

7. To add the items back in simply uncomment the code.

Question 90: Updating List IDs

How do you update the list IDs in the database when migrating sites with data views?

A: When using sites with data views and migrating them to different environments, you're presented with two problems.

The list IDs referenced in the data views are from the original environment.

When the site is restored using migrate all the List IDs are updated to different IDs. This means that if you have a data view that is referencing the old List IDs you'll get an error that the List doesn't exist. This can really be a pain when you have lots of data views on your site.

Below is an SQL Script that will copy over the correct List IDs from the previous database to ensure your data views work correctly.

1. Open Enterprise Manager.

2. Create a Temp database.

3. Import your original database into the Temp database.

4. Use the script below. Be sure to change all references of the Temp and actual Content Database. The script below will also check for duplicate IDs as well to ensure it doesn't overwrite any existing lists. The likelihood of this happening is slim to none. When the script is done, browse to your site and the data views will display the proper data.

*/

```
-- Declare variables

DECLARE @ListTitle varchar(255)

DECLARE @FromListID varchar(36)

DECLARE @ToListID varchar(36)

DECLARE @SameIDCount int

/*

Table Names to Update

Add additional lines if necessary to accommodate all lists
on your site.

*/

/* CONFIG: Lists and Libraries */

--SET @ListTitle = 'LISTNAME 1'

--SET @ListTitle = 'LISTNAME 2'

--SET @ListTitle = 'LISTNAME 3'

/*  End */

/*
```

The following statement retrieves the "From" database
WSS list ID and assigns it to the "From" variable:

```
*/

-- CONFIG: Name of "From" site WSS content DB

USE [FROM_DATABASE]

SELECT @FromListID = Lists.tp_ID

FROM Lists

WHERE tp_Title = @ListTitle

/*
```

The following statement sets the SameIDCount variable to 1 in the unlikely event that an identical content ID has been assigned by WSS in the "To" site.

```
*/
USE [TO_DATABASE]
IF (SELECT COUNT(*) FROM Lists
WHERE tp_ID = @FromListID) > 0
  SET @SameIDCount = 1
ELSE
  SET @SameIDCount = 0
/*
```

The following statement retrieves the "To" database WSS list ID and assigns it to the "To" variable.

```
*/
-- CONFIG: Name of "To" site WSS content DB
USE [TO_DATABASE]
-- Get "To" list ID
SELECT @ToListID = Lists.tp_ID
FROM Lists
WHERE tp_Title = @ListTitle
/*
```

The following statement updates the "Lists" table in the "To" site's WSS content database with the old content ID if no duplicate exists.

```
*/
-- CONFIG: Name of "To" site WSS content DB
USE [TO_DATABASE]
```

```
IF @SameIDCount = 0

UPDATE Lists

SET tp_ID = @FromListID

WHERE tp_Title = @ListTitle

/*
```

The following statement updates all content in the "Docs" table in the "To" site's WSS content Database with the old content ID if no duplicate exists.

```
*/

-- CONFIG: Name of "To" site WSS content DB

USE [TO_DATABASE]

IF @SameIDCount = 0

UPDATE Docs

SET ListId = @FromListID

WHERE ListId = @ToListID

/*
```

The following statement updates all content in the "WebParts" table in the "To" site's WSS content database with the old content ID if no duplicate exists.

```
*/

-- CONFIG: Name of "To" site WSS content DB

USE [TO_DATABASE]

IF @SameIDCount = 0

UPDATE WebParts

SET tp_ListID = @FromListID

WHERE tp_ListID = @ToListID

/*
```

The following statement updates all content in the
"UserData" table in the "To" site's WSS content database
with the old content ID if no duplicate exists.

```
*/
-- CONFIG: Name of "To" site WSS content DB
USE [TO_DATABASE]
IF @SameIDCount = 0
UPDATE UserData
SET tp_ListID = @FromListID
WHERE tp_ListID = @ToListID
```

Question 91: Installing Share Point Portal Server 2003

How do you install Share Point Portal Server 2003,
Windows Share Point Services, and Project Server 2003 on
the same server?

A: Although installing the programs that are listed in the
"Applies to" section on the same server may be a good
testing environment, we do not recommend this practice if
a company is going to use these services to their fullest
capacity.

Microsoft Office Share Point Portal Server 2003 is very
CPU intensive with its crawling and indexing functions.
Microsoft Office Project Server 2003 is just as intensive for
its publishing and VW notify services.

Note running these services at the same time on the same server may create conflicts. For example, some of the conflicts that may occur include:

1. Excessive memory usage.
2. Excessive paging to the hard disk drive.
3. Service performance degradation.
4. One service delaying the start of the other service.

Question 92: Creating Links List

How do you create a links list and have the links open in a new window?

A: One of the most requested customizations of Share Point is making the links list items open in a new window. In the web world this can happen several different ways, with JavaScript, or a simple 'target=' attribute added the 'a' tag. Share Point data views render data in XSL from XML. XSL is like CSS for HTML, but applies only to XML.

Below are steps that will walk you through creating a links list out of a custom list and then changing the code to have the links open in a new window.

1. Create a Custom List.

2. Modify the Settings and Columns.

3. Add the following fields:

> a) Title (Required)
> This should be a standard text box.

> b) Description (Optional)

> This is optional but helps in search results. This can either be a simple text box or multilane text box.

> c) URL (Required)
> This should be a standard text box.

Once the custom list is created, add a few line items to the list to populate it. Once the list is populated, please continue following the directions below.

1. Open the site in FrontPage.

2. Open the page where you would like the list to reside (data view).

3. Add a Web Part Zone to your new page if one already doesn't exist.

4. Click Insert.

5. Insert Data view.

6. Select your links list and click Insert Data view.

7. Remove all the columns except for the Title.

8. Switch FrontPage to the Code view (located at the bottom of the page).

9. Search for '<a href=".

10. Change your '<a>' tag to look like the one below.

<a href="{@URL}" target="_blank"><xsl:value-of

11. Select="@Title"/></a>.

The XSL:value-of-select="@Title" may change depending on the name of the field. To view this, right click the field in your data view and select "Copy X-Path."

12. Paste your x-Path copy into note pad and @ the property will be displayed.

Question 93: Content Editor Web Part

How do I make the Content Editor Web Part searchable?

A: You can do the following:

1. Search the Setup and Configuration.

2. Add a Full-Text Catalog to SQL Server.

3. Open Enterprise Manager.

4. Expand the server group containing the site's content database and then expand the server.

5. Expand the Content Database.

6. "Right" click, select "New," and then click "New Full-Text Catalog."

7. Assign a name to your catalog using the convention FulltextUpdate_<Content_Database_Name) (e.g. FullTextUpdate_SiteName).
In the Full-Text Catalog wizard, click on the "Schedules" tab.

8. Click "New Catalog Schedule."

9. Enter a name for the full text catalog, e.g., FullTextUpdate_SiteName_Schedule.

10. Select "Full Population."

11. Select "Recurring" and click on "Change."

12. Select "Daily" and set the time to be 12:30 a.m. (NOTE: This is very important because the table update has to run first before the Index Catalog can grab new content.)

13. Click "OK." A message will appear stating the connection was successful.
Click "OK."

14. Create and Populate the CEW_Search Table.

15. Open SQL Query Analyzer and Connect to the SQL Server where the table will be created.

16. Using Query Analyzer, open the "Combined CEW_SEARCH TABLE CREATE 0.0.1.sql" script.

IMPORTANT: In the script, please check to make sure the correct database is referenced. This is the first line of code and starts with "Use." Search for "CONFIG:" to find the "USE" statement that needs to be updated.

17. Execute the script.

18. Verify that the CEW_Search table has been created in the content database via Enterprise Manager.

19. Connect All Website Catalogs to the CEW_Search Table.

20. Open Enterprise Manager.

21. Expand the server group containing the site's content database and then expand the server.

22. Expand the Content database.

23. Right click on the CEW_Search table and select "Full-Text Index Table."

25. "Define Full-Text Indexing on a Table."

26. Click "Next" at the welcome message.

27. Click "Next" on "Unique Index."

29. Select "Data" and "LeafName" from the "Available Columns" field.

30. Click "Next."

31. Select the Newly Create Catalog (CEW_Search).

32. Click "Next."

33. Do not assign a schedule because a schedule is already created during the Catalog creation process.

34. Click "Next."

35. Click "Finish."

36. Click "OK."

37. Update the table when content changes occur.

38. Open SQL Query Analyzer and Connect to the SQL Server where the table will be created.

39. Open the script "Combined CEW_SEARCH TABLE JOB UPDATE 0.0.1.sql."

IMPORTANT: In the script please check to make sure the correct database is referenced. This is a line of code and starts with "Use." Type in the name of the database where the table will reside. The job and the database being reflected in the script will also be updated:

```
-- CONFIG:  Assign the JobName, DBOwner, and Database Name

SET @JobName = 'CEW_SearchUpdate'

SET @DBOwner = 'sa'

SET @Database = 'CONTENT_DATABASE'

-- END CONFIG
```

Once the job name and database names are changed execute the script.

Repeat steps 1 – 3, uncomment the appropriate blocks for each site.

Update the CEW_Search Table

Open Enterprise Manager.

Expand the target SQL Server environment.

Expand the Management Section.

Expand SQL Server Agent.

Click on "Jobs."

Right click on a job and select "Start Job."

Right click on the job again and select "View Job History" to verify that the job ran successfully.

Update the Index.

Open Enterprise Manager.

Expand the target SQL Server environment.

Expand "Databases" and then select the Content database.

Click on "Full-Text Catalogs."

Right click on the CEW_Search catalog.

Select "Full Population."

Click "OK."

After creating the database and populating the table, the search page will have to be developed or the search.aspx page in Windows Share Point Services will have to be modified to show the new table in the results. Below is a ZIP file containing the SQL Scripts needed.

Question 94: Removing "Mail To"

How do I remove the "mail to:" when copying Excel email addresses?

A: When copying email addresses from one datasheet to another the email addresses change and adds the mail to: in the text next to the email. This isn't bad and the email address will still work when clicked by a user, however, it doesn't look that appealing and wastes screen real estate. Below are steps on how to remove the mail to: text all at once instead of by line.

1. Browse to the list.

2. Export the list to Excel.

3. Click Open, Don't Save the List.

4. Click Edit, Replace.

In the Find What text box enter in mail to:

5. Click Find Next.

6. Click Replace to make sure it replaces the mail to: with nothing.

7. Click Replace All.

8. Click Synchronize List.

9. Close Excel, Don't Save unless you want to.

10. Refresh your browser and the email addresses should change.

Question 95: Changing Personal Information

How do you change your personal information?

A: By default Share Point will display 'domain\username' in the fields related to who was last participating in a document, list, survey, etc.

To change from 'domain\username' to show your actual name follow the instructions below:

1. Log into the Portal.

2. Click the Welcome domain\username in the upper right hand corner. A drop down menu will appear

3. Click My Settings.

4. Click Edit Item .

5. Change your Name field and fill in any additional fields as necessary .

6. Click OK.

7. To verify your name has changed look at the Welcome message. It should say "Welcome Your Name" instead of your domain\username.

Question 96: Displaying PDF Icon

How to display a PDF icon in a document library?

A: You may have noticed that when uploading a PDF to a document library, that the default image is displayed. Follow these steps to see the PDF icon in your document libraries and also how to add it to the Share Point file system.

Obtain a PDF icon of your choice:

1. Rename the image icpdf.gif.

2. Copy the image to this directory drive letter: `\program files\common files\microsoft shared\web server extensions\60\template\images` on each front-end web server.

3. Edit the docicon.xml file located in drive letter: `\program files\common files\microsoft shared\web server extensions\60\template\xml folder.`

4. Add this code to your docicon.xml file `<Mapping Key="pdf" Value="icpdf.gif"/>`

5. Restart IIS.

6. Click Start.

7. Run.

8. Type IISRESET.

9. Press Enter.

Note: When screen disappears IIS has reset, browse to a document library with a PDF document. If you don't see the document, click Refresh (F5).

Question 97: Using Web Services to Display Information

How do I use web services to display information?

A: One great feature of using FrontPage 2003 and its integration with Share Point is that you can use SOAP data queries to show lists and libraries on the same or different sites.

The instructions below cover adding a data view using the Web Services available in Share Point.

1. Open this subsite in FrontPage.

2. Browse to http://myserver/subsite/default.aspx and click File > Edit in Microsoft FrontPage, or Launch FrontPage and click File > Open Site and type in this URL.

3. Open the default.aspx page if it isn't open already Data..Insert Data View (this should launch the Data Source Catalog).

4. At the bottom of the Catalog, expand "XML Web Services." Click "Add to catalog."

5. Type in this URL: http://myserver/_vti_bin/lists.asmx

6. Click "Connect now."

7. In the "Operation" drop-down, change the value to "GetListItems" method.

8. Change the listName property to "Announcements" (without the quotes).

9. Click OK.

10. Right click this data source and choose "Show Data" (should launch the Data View Details taskpane).

11. Select the fields you want to display.

12. Place the Cursor in the page where you want to insert the Data View.
Click "Insert Data View" from the taskpane.
From the Data..Style menu, you can control the appearance, paging, toolbars, etc.
From the Data..Filter menu, you can add a filter for the data source.
From the Data..Web Part Properties dialog, you can control the web part chrome.

By going into code view, you can add the JavaScript to enable the drop-down menu items for editing the list items, if that's what you want. You can also use FrontPage's design tools to create hyperlinks. For example:

1. Select the title data value.

2. Insert > Hyperlink.

3. Create a hyperlink to the editform.aspx page.

4. Click on Parameters.

5. Add a parameter to the URL for the List ID number.

6. OK back to the page.

That should allow you to click on the Title and edit that specific list item.

Question 98: Office 2003 Error

We have noticed that Share Point lists can only be viewed when it has Office 2003 pro installed.

If it is Office 2003 standards they get this message:

```
"A datasheet component compatible with Windows Share Point
Services is
Not installed.

Your web browser does not support ActiveX controls
Support for ActiveX controls is disabled."
```

What do we need to do to a user's machine if they get this message?

Can this ActiveX control be installed from somewhere for people who get this error?

A: Microsoft has left a very easy backdoor to make Office 2003 Standard Edition work with Share Point 2003, which is nothing but the presence/absence of a special registry key.

Start Registry Editor & navigate to: Hkey Local Machine --> Software --> Microsoft --> Office --> 11.0 --> Common --> Product Version

1. On the left pane, highlight the Node "Product Version", right click --> New--> "Binary Value."

2. Give it the value name "ProInfo."

3. Give it the value data 0000 0001.

4. Now reboot the machine.

5. Now open a browser and launch any Share Point List and try to view it in Datasheet View.

It will work fine even on a machine with Office 2003 Standard Edition.

DISCLAIMER:
There is enough reason to believe that this registry tweak falls outside the legal norms laid out by Microsoft. You are advised to carry this out at your own risk.

Please restrain from using this solution on your corporate network and office machines. Doing so can invite legal action by Microsoft, which may amount to termination of service of employees found responsible, as per your company's IT Policy.

Question 99: Background Image

How do I make a background image display on every page?

A: This will cover editing the correct style elements and their attributes in the OWS and SPS cascading style sheets. These style sheets can be located on each of your front end web servers in this location drive letter: \program files\common files\Microsoft shared\web server extensions\60\template\layouts\1033\styles. Once you locate the files you will need to either use FrontPage 2003 or a compatible text editor to make changes to the files.

1. Make a copy of the original OWS.CSS file.

2. Open OWS.CSS.

3. Find .ms-main. This element handles the look and feel for the main portal table.

4. Replace current code with code below:

```
.ms-main

{

background-position: center; background-image:

url('/_layouts/images/image.gif'); background-repeat: no-
repeat;

}
```

5. Save the file.

6. Copy your image into the images directory located on the all of the front-end web servers drive letter:

```
\program files\common files\Microsoft shared\web server
```

`extensions\60\template\images.`

7. Browse to your site and refresh your page.

The "background-repeat: no-repeat" will make the image display only in the center of the page. You can change its value to have the background repeat or simply remove that attribute to have the image repeat.

Question 100: Changing Network Passwords

How do I allow users to change their network passwords via Share Point?

A: This will explain using the IIS Admin Password changing pages available and linking them to Share Point.

1. Open IIS.

2. Create a New Virtual Server under the main Share Point Site.

3. Call the Virtual Server "Change Password."

4. Browse to this folder where the .ASP pages are held [drive letter]:\Windows\System32\inetsrv\isadmpwd.

5. Open Share Point Central Administrator.

6. Click Configure Virtual Server Settings.

7. Click the Site Name.

8. Click Define Managed Paths.

In the Path text box type in the name of the new subdirectory that was just created "Change Password/" Under Type select Excluded Path -- Excluding the path will allow IIS to display the ASP pages.
Test the new Virtual Server Pages.

9. Open IIS.

10. Click the "+" sign next to the Website where the Virtual Directory was created.

11. Select Change Password.
In the Right hand column, Right Click AEXP2.ASP and select Browse.
The Change Password Page will appear.
With the Change Password Page appearing this guarantees users will be able to browse to page via a browser.

Adding the Pages to the Share Point Interface:

1. Open up your site in a browser.

2. Add a new Content Editor Web Part to the page of your choice.

3. Edit the Content Editor Web Part.

4. Name it Change Password.
Under Appearance, Frame Style, Select None.

5. Click Source Editor.
Type in the following code:

```
<a href="/change password/aexp2.asp">Change Password</a>
```

6. Click Save.

7. Click OK.

Note: In the <a href> tag you can make this open in a new windows by specifying a target for example, <a href="/change password/aexp2.asp" target="_blank">Change Password</a>.

At this point a new link should be displayed on the page called "Change Password." When the link is clicked the IIS Password Change screen should appear allowing users to change their passwords. The Username/Domain should be profiled with what they logged in with. The page can be exported and saved to import into other sites or pages if needed.

ACKNOWLEDGEMENTS:

http://www.devx.com/dotnet/Article/27673

http://forums.asp.net/thread/1116952.aspx

http://james.wss.bcentral.com/sharepoint/default.aspx

http://www.tek-tips.com/threadminder.cfm?pid=820

http://msd2d.com/default_section.aspx?section=sharepoint

http://www.sharepointu.com/forums/default.asp

Index